INDEPENDENT AND UNOFFICIAL
MINECRAFT
STEM CHALLENGE
BUILD A THEME PARK
T0019599

THIS IS A CARLTON BOOK

Published in 2018 by Carlton Books Limited
An imprint of the Carlton Publishing Group
20 Mortimer Street, London W1T 3JW

A catalogue record for this book is available from the British Library.

ISBN: 978-1-78312-405-3

Printed in China
3 5 7 9 10 8 6 4

Designed and packaged by:
Dynamo Limited

Built by Darcy Myles and written by Anne Rooney

The publishers would like to thank the following sources for their kind permission to reproduce the pictures in the book.

Key: t = top, b = bottom, c = centre, l = left & r = right

18c. St-fotograf/Shutterstock, 18b Africa Studio/Shutterstock, 18br ra3rn/Shutterstock, 22l Tarica/Shutterstock, 22r Nixx Photography/Shutterstock, 24cr MagMac83/Shutterstock, 24br PhotoRoman/Shutterstock, 30l KZWW/Shutterstock, 30r Kazitafahnizeer/Shutterstock, 32l Loraks/Shutterstock, 38. Lisa S./Shutterstock, 40c Dudarev Mikhail/Shutterstock, 40b RDFlemming/Shutterstock, 46l SAPhotog/Shutterstock, 46r Getty Images, 48 Stokkete/Shutterstock

Every effort has been made to acknowledge correctly and contact the source and/or copyright holder of each picture, and Carlton Publishing Group apologizes for any unintentional errors or omissions, which will be corrected in future editions of this book.

THEME PARK

INDEPENDENT AND UNOFFICIAL

MINECRAFT STEM CHALLENGE

BUILD A THEME PARK

CONTENTS

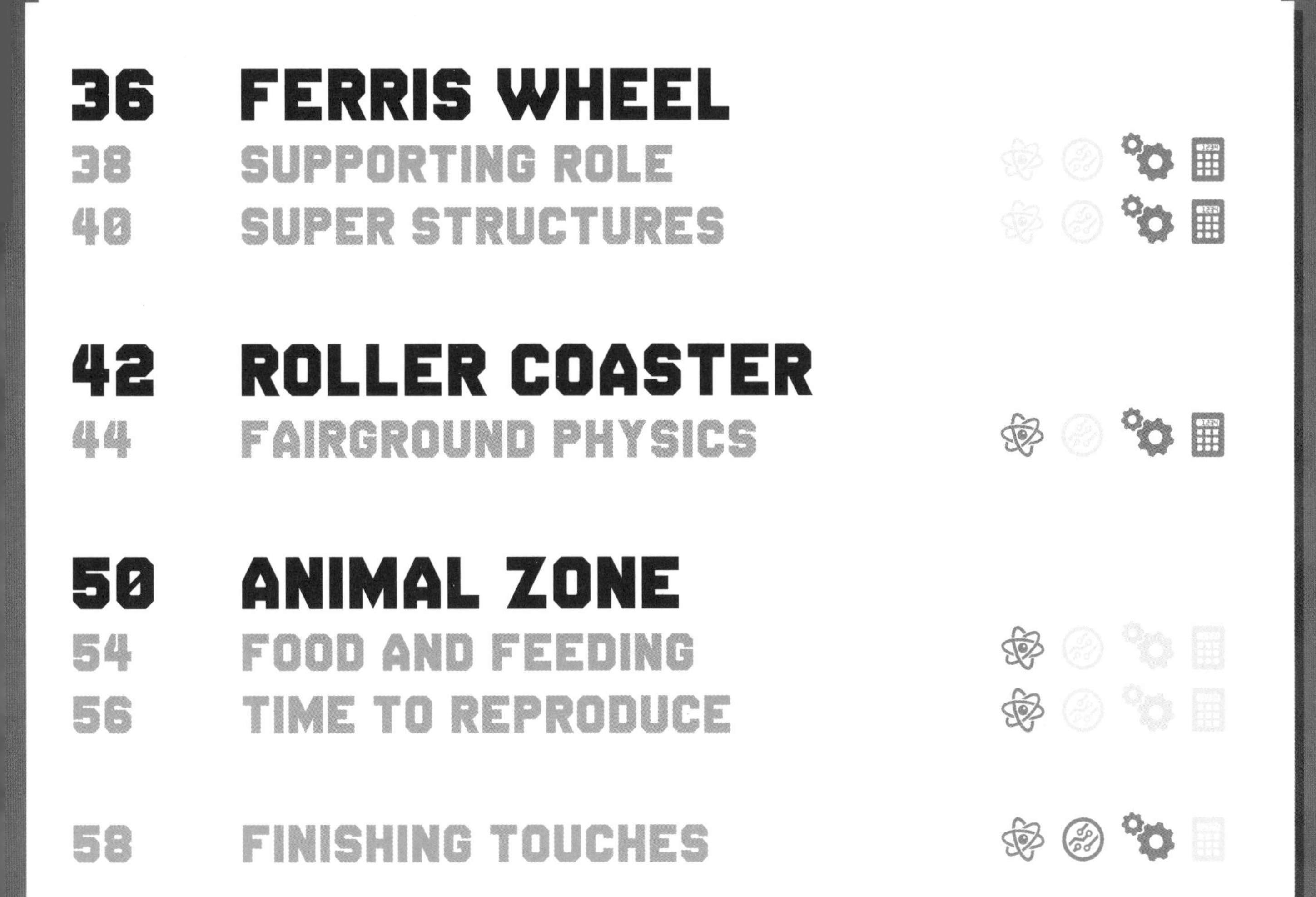

SCIENCE
TECHNOLOGY
ENGINEERING
MATHS

WELCOME TO THE THEME PARK!

In this book we'll show you how to build a fantastic Minecraft theme park with all the attractions of a real-life park, such as a Ferris wheel, a bouncy castle and a roller coaster. If you're ready to have fun, let's start building!

AND HERE'S HOW IT LOOKS FROM ABOVE!

We've put the builds in an order that has the easier ones first, but you don't have to do them in that order. As long as you stick to the plan on page 11, and you make the paths and fences first that divide up the areas, you can build the rides in any order and the theme park will fit together perfectly.

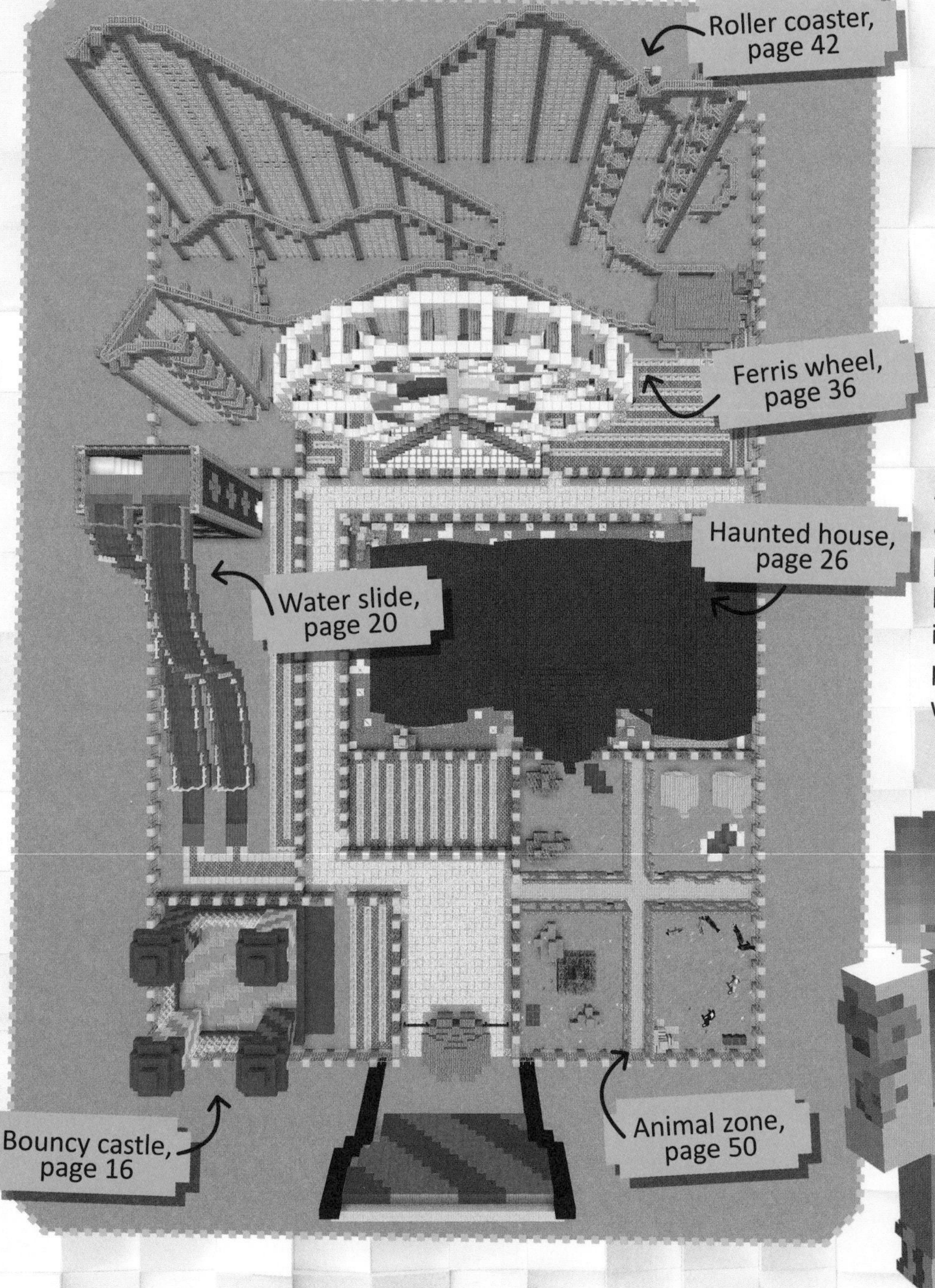

DOING MORE

We don't want to limit your imagination! Use the book as your starting point and make an enormous theme park, if you like. If you want to add more things, either wait until you've finished or add them outside the area covered by the plan. For instance, if you want to create a rink for bumper cars, you might put it behind the roller coaster. All you'll have to do then is adjust the fence around the park to include your new bit. But if you put new items in the area covered by the plan, you'll find the builds won't all fit.

GETTING CREATIVE

If you've only used Minecraft in Survival mode before, you'll be used to having to collect building materials and tools and avoid all kinds of perils to stay alive. Building is a matter of survival and you might have settled for a hut to protect you. If you want to focus on building super structures, you can make life much easier for yourself by working in Creative mode. There will be no hostile mobs out to get you, and you'll have endless supplies of all the materials you want.

IT'S A FLAT, FLAT WORLD

It's pretty hard to build a theme park in the mountains or underwater. Luckily, Minecraft lets you choose a perfectly flat world for building so you don't have to struggle with the wrong type of landscape. Here's how to do it:

Superflat world

STEP 1

At the Select World screen, choose Create New World.

STEP 2

Give your new world a name, then click on the Game Mode button twice until it shows Game Mode: Creative.

STEP 3

Click on the button More World Options.

STEP 4

Click on the World Type button to show the option World Type: Superflat.

STEP 5

Click Done, and then Create New World. Your new world will start with unending views of green grass beneath a blue sky. Time to get building!

STAYING SAFE ONLINE

Minecraft is one of the most popular games in the world, and we want you to have fun while you're playing it. However, it is just as important to stay safe when you're online.

Top tips for staying safe are:

- turn off chat
- find a child-friendly server
- watch out for viruses and malware
- set a game-play time limit
- tell a trusted adult what you're doing.

Courtesy of IAmNewAsWell

CHOOSING MATERIALS

In Creative mode, you don't need to hunt for materials or dig them out of the ground. They are available all the time. Press the E key to bring up the Building Blocks menu. You can pick up to nine materials to have readily to hand and there's no limit to the number of blocks you can use.

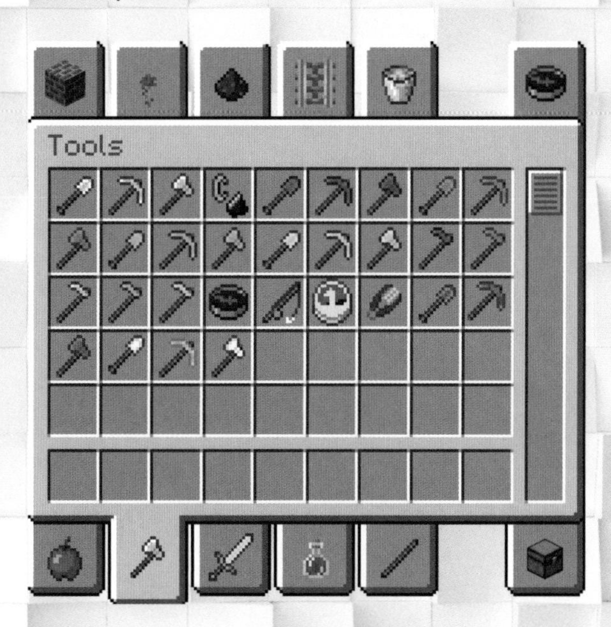

GOOD FOUNDATIONS

In real life, buildings aren't plonked straight on top of the ground — they would fall down. They have foundations underground to keep them solid and stable. In a real theme park, the structures would have poles and pillars going deep into the ground so that they would not fall or blow over and cause accidents. In Minecraft, we don't need to worry about foundations.

ON THE GROUND

This plan shows the areas set aside for the different builds. As long as you follow it carefully, your theme park will come together perfectly.

ONE STEP AT A TIME

The area on the ground that is occupied by a build is called its footprint. Sometimes, the footprint is larger than the bottom layer of the build. If there is an overhang (a wider section further up), we need to leave space underneath.

PLANS AND MEASUREMENTS

Architects, quantity surveyors and builders work to detailed plans. They use a consistent scale so that they can work out the measurements for all the parts of what they are building. For example, a plan might have a scale of 1:100, which would mean that each 1 cm measured on the plan corresponds with 100 cm (1 metre) in the actual building.

PERIMETER AND AREA

The perimeter is the total distance around a shape. The theme park's perimeter is the total length of its four sides:

124 + 83 + 124 + 83 = 414 blocks.

As it's a line, perimeter has one dimension.

The area of a shape is the space it covers. As the theme park is a rectangle, its area is the length of the long side multiplied by the length of the short side:

124 x 83 = 10,292 blocks.

Area has two dimensions, so it's usually reported in 'square' units, such as square centimetres (cm^2) or square metres (m^2).

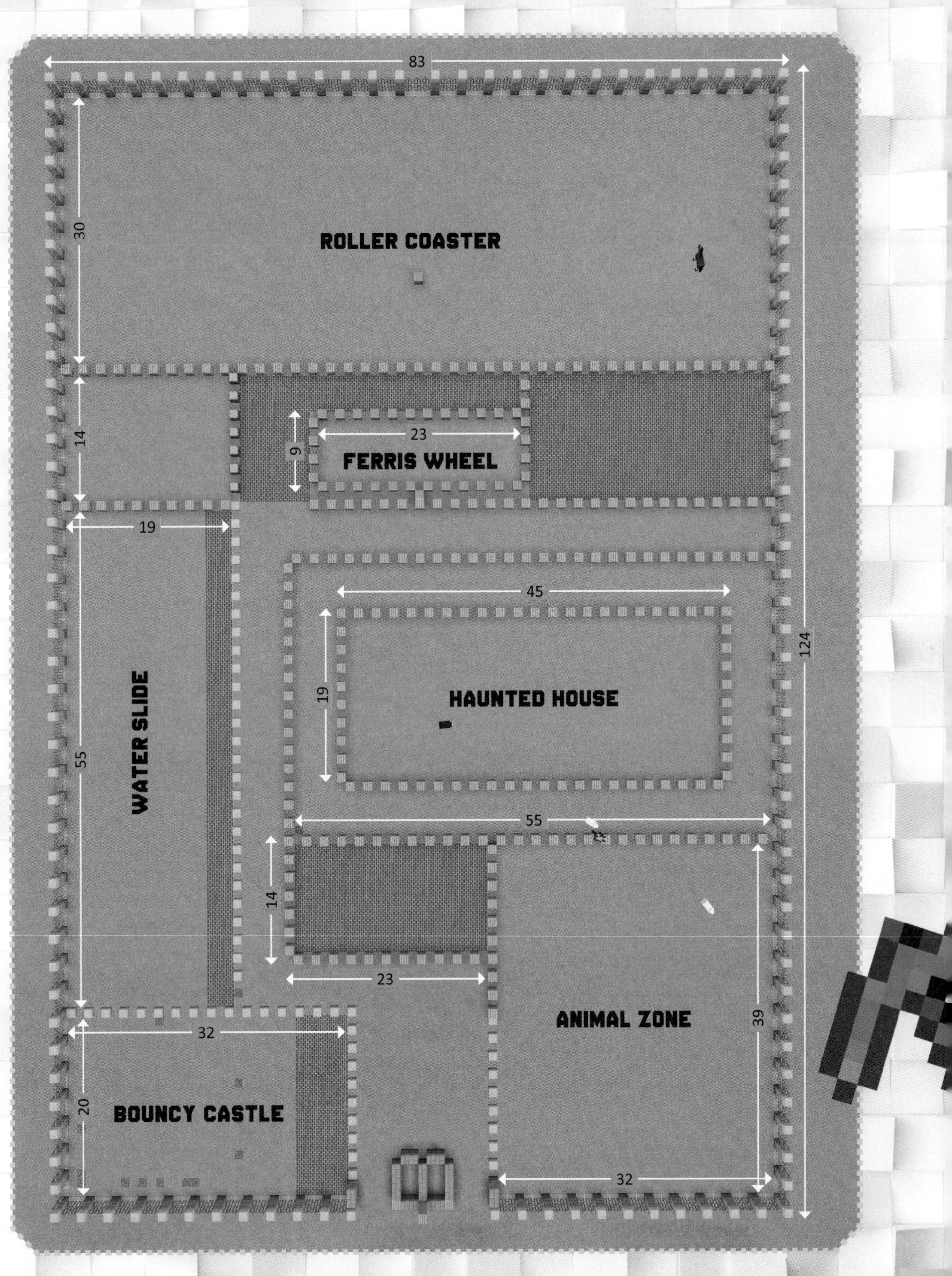
83
124
30
ROLLER COASTER
14
9
23
FERRIS WHEEL
19
45
19
HAUNTED HOUSE
WATER SLIDE
55
55
14
23
ANIMAL ZONE
39
32
32
20
BOUNCY CASTLE
32

SETTING THE SCENE

We'll start by marking out all the areas for each build and laying paving. In real life, surveyors also work out exactly where everything is going to go. Marking the boundaries between rides at this stage makes it easy to see where to start each build.

THEME PARK

GRIDLOCK

The plan on page 11 shows shows how much space you will need for each ride. This type of plan is similar to ones that real builders, architects and designers use. It helps you to see how all the different parts of the theme park fit together. There is a more detailed plan at the start of each build so that you can easily see what sizes to make all the parts.

STEP 1

Begin by marking out the perimeter of the theme park. Dig up grass blocks and replace them with polished andesite to create a 124x83 rectangle. Knock out a gap in the middle of one short side for the entrance. The gap should be 15 blocks wide, with 34 blocks on either side of it.

STEP 2

Now make a fence around the perimeter. The fence has pillars made of two blocks of stone brick with a stone slab on top. Build pillars in each corner, leave two slabs empty, then add another pillar. Keep going all the way round. Then fill in the gaps with iron bars.

STEP 3

Using the plan on page 11 as a guide, mark out the areas for the different rides, using any blocks you like. This will help you to count up the blocks more easily for each build.

STEP 4

The areas of red paving which you can see in the plan on page 11 are level with the ground, so you will need to dig out a layer one block deep before adding bricks. Double-check the dimensions by counting the blocks: it's important that you get these right so that there's enough space for each build.

STEP 5

Add the 6x7 footprint for the ticket booths using stone brick and oak wood plank.

MATERIAL WORLD

Materials have different properties. In Minecraft you can build a bouncy castle from wool or a water slide from pink clay, which would never work in the real world.

You don't have to make your theme park look just like ours. You can use different colours and materials. As long as you stick to the basic structure and dimensions so that it all fits and works in the space, you can change the decorations. Your water ride could be a lava ride. Your haunted house could have a track running through it. You could give your whole park a theme through its colours and decorations: Hallowe'en, fairyland, fantasy or sci-fi. It can be anything you like.

TOP TIP!

Using materials that would work in the real world makes your builds look more realistic.

carved pumpkin

lava block

Courtesy of 'Cornbass'

ROCK, METAL, WOOD

In the real world, buildings are made from lots of different materials. Some of the most common types are:

- brick and concrete
- stone (and slate for roofs)
- wood
- metal

You can use all these in Minecraft, too, so it's worth learning a bit about their properties.

bricks

Brick, stone and concrete are super-hard and strong. Buildings made of these materials don't easily fall down, are not damaged by weather, and don't burn. But they're also heavy, and quite difficult to work with because they are so hard. Bricks and concrete are made in factories, and stone is cut from the ground.

polished granite

stone brick

Wood is light, easy to work with and easy to find – it grows on trees! Wood is flammable (it can catch fire). Over time, wood can rot while structures made from brick, stone and concrete can last for centuries.

In Minecraft, wood comes in blocks, stairs, planks and slabs, and also forms other items such as fences and doors. Minecraft also offers different types of wood.

oak wood plank

wooden door

Metal is strong, but flexible. At high temperatures it melts, but it doesn't burn. We usually use metal for the support structures inside buildings made of concrete or brick. Metals conduct electricity and some are magnetic.

oak fence

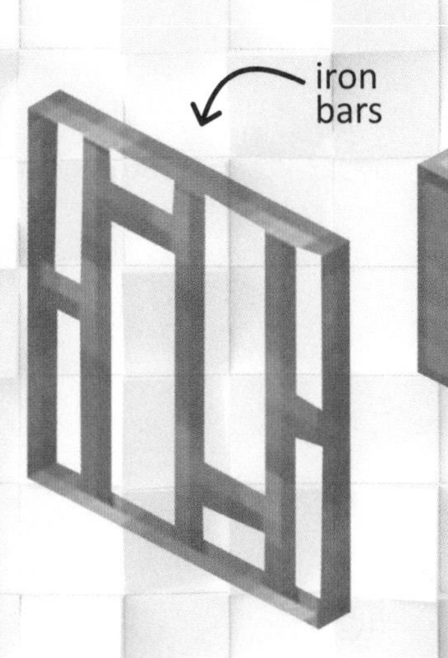

iron block

oak wood stair

BOUNCY CASTLE

What could be more fun than bouncing sky-high on a multi-coloured castle? This one is just inside the entrance to your theme park, and it's a great first build.

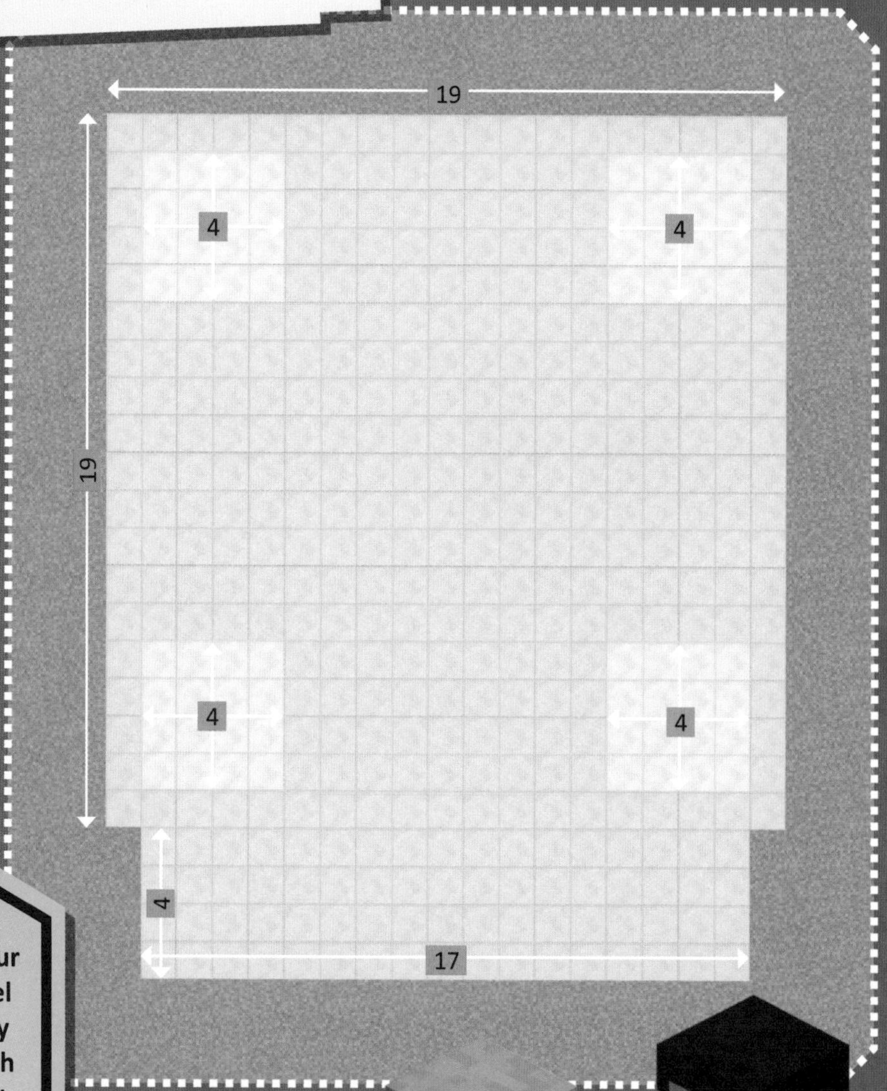

19

19

4

4

4

4

4

17

GETTING STARTED

Here's the layout for your bouncy castle. Look carefully at the plan and refer back to it as you are building. It has all the dimensions you will need to use. The plan is shown to scale. Your build will have exactly the same proportions as the picture in the plan.

UNREAL!

In Minecraft, slime is bouncy. Your customers might not like the feel of a bouncy castle made entirely of slime, so we've covered it with wool, which is nice and soft — it feels much nicer than slime. The slime will be bouncy, even when it's covered with wool.

Alex and Steve (your customers)

STEP 1

Mark out a square 19x19 blocks. Go all around the perimeter laying a single row of red wool. Now fill in the middle with a single layer of slime – it's what will give your bouncy castle its boing!

TOP TIP!

People need to be safe in your theme park. You don't want them to bounce right off the bouncy castle, so we've put a soft landing area at the front.

STEP 2

Dig out a rectangle 17x4 as a landing area to one side. It starts one block in from the edge of the bouncy base. Fill it with a layer of red wool. This is a soft landing area in case anyone bounces right off.

STEP 3

Build four 4x4 bases for the towers in each corner using coloured wool. Create a barrier between the tower bases by adding a row of red wool along three sides. Fill in the middle with wool in any colours and patterns you like. The slime will still be bouncy, but it's nicer to bounce on wool than on slime.

IMPORTANT STUFF

Materials can be used to control how we physically feel. They can be used to control light, temperature and even the way we move so that we are more comfortable and secure.

BOUNCY MATERIALS

A real bouncy castle is not made of slime and wool. It's made of a rubbery plastic material and it's inflatable. It is filled with air using a giant pump. As you jump on it, the pressure of your body pressing down squeezes some of the air out of the way from underneath you. But it can't go far as the bouncy castle is already full of air. This means you sink a bit, but the air inside pushes back up, too, making it bouncy.

Your feet push down, the trapped air pushes back – and you bounce!

WARM AND WOOLY

A material like wool that is warm to the touch is a thermal insulator. This means that heat doesn't travel through it easily. That's why a woolly jumper is good for keeping you warm: the heat of your body can't travel through the wool to the outside air. Materials that are cold to the touch, like metal, are thermal conductors. Metal feels cold because it carries heat away from your body.

The plastic handle on a frying pan doesn't conduct heat – no need to protect your hands.

A metal baking tray conducts heat so you have to wear oven gloves.

STEP 4

Build each of your towers ten blocks high. Use any colours and patterns you like. Leave one block missing from the top corner of each tower – this shape will help you form the base of the turrets you are going to build next.

STEP 5

For your turrets, place a 2x2 square of red wool in each corner of the tower. These will fill the missing blocks and stick out around to the top of the tower. Join these together by placing rows of four blocks above them. Finish off with a 4x4 square and a 2x2 square on top.

STEP 6

Finally, on top of the red wool edges of the castle, add a barrier of cobweb three blocks high. Build up the ends by adding an L-shape made from three cobweb blocks. Cobweb is just the right material to use for a protective barrier, as people can see through it but not bounce through it.

Staggering blocks creates shadows and breaks up the... well, blockiness of Minecraft!

WATER SLIDE

After all that bouncing, your visitors might want to cool off with a bit of a splash. A water slide is great on a warm day — you're bound to get at least a little bit wet!

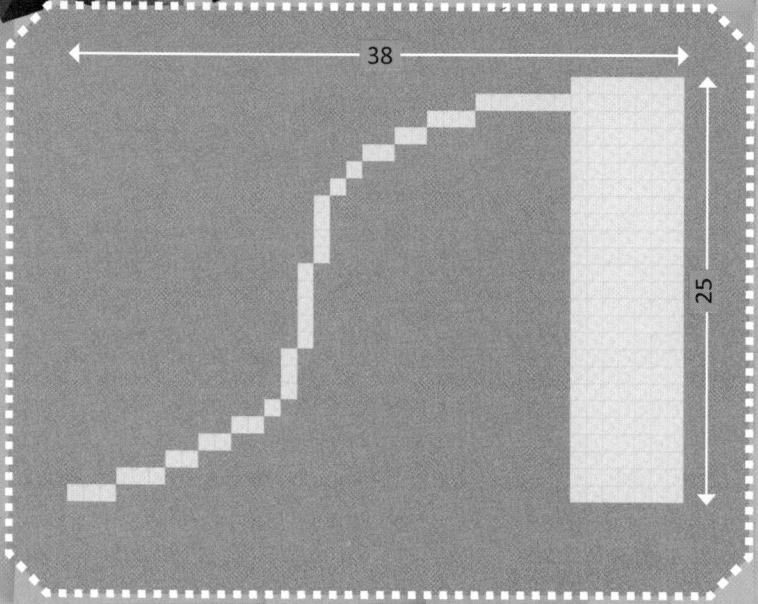

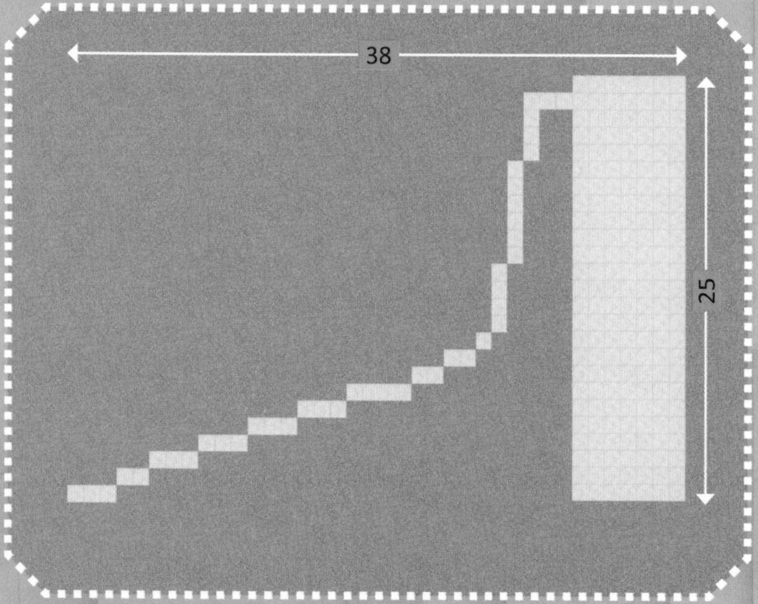

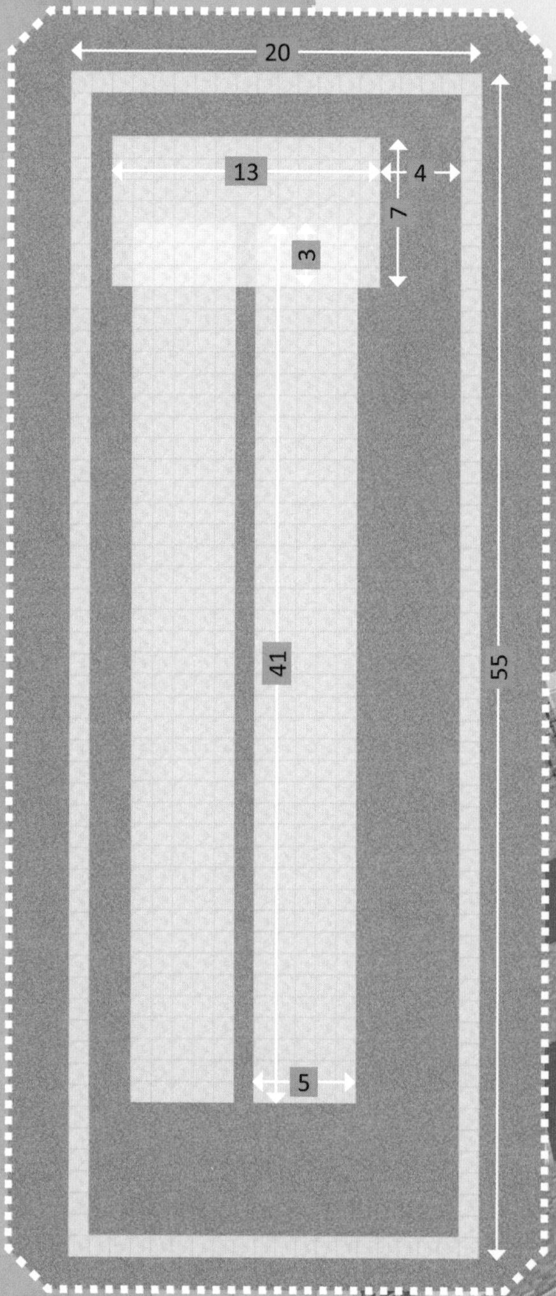

LOCATION, LOCATION

The water slide is just behind the bouncy castle. Look carefully at the theme park plan on page 11 and refer back to it as you are building. Make sure you build it in the right place and facing the right way: the water slides come down towards the bouncy castle so visitors can see their friends bouncing as they hurtle downwards.

SHAPE AND SPEED

The shape of a surface and what it is made of affect the speed at which objects – and even air and water – can move over it.

CURVING IN AND OUT

The curves of the slides go in different directions, one bowing outwards and one inwards:

The convex curve on this mirror gives drivers a wider view.

We can say that a curve bowing outwards is convex and one bowing inwards is concave. But whether a curve is convex or concave depends on which side of it you are standing.

One way round this is to call the curves 'concave upwards' and 'concave downwards' (or convex downwards and convex upwards!). The magenta slide is concave downwards; the blue slide is concave upwards.

FAST AND SLOW

Going down these two slides would be very different! People on the water slide will go fastest where the slope is steepest, so on the magenta ride they will start slowly and then really speed up, and on the blue slide they will go super-fast straight away. Which would you rather do?

The concave curve on this spoon helps it hold liquid.

UNDER AND OVER

Although the tower and the end of the slide are on the ground, much of the slide is elevated so there is empty space underneath it. On the plan, this space is still shown as part of its layout (the area it occupies) so no one puts a tall sign or lamppost there. The tower has steps inside so that visitors can go up, and windows to let some light in – you don't want them to trip on the stairs.

READY STEADY

We're going to begin by building the framework so that you can see the general shape of the waterslide, and then we'll fill it in. Look at the theme park footprint to make sure you start in the right place.

STEP 1

Count out a 7x13 rectangle one block in from the perimeter fence and the back of the water slide section of the plan. This will be the base for your wooden tower. Place a 25x1 oak wood column in each corner. Join up the tops of the columns on each short side of the rectangle. Use the plans on page 20 to help you build the base for each slide from magenta (which looks pink) and light blue hardened clay (which looks purple). At the end of your slides, dig out 5x3x2 blocks of soil and line them with clay for the water to drain into. Add some more clay blocks at the end to finish off.

STEP 2

It would be good to see some water flowing, so let's take advantage of the magic of the Minecraft world and add it now! Add sides to each slide first so that the water will flow in the right direction and not down the sides of the slides. Then add a water bucket at the top of each slide. Minecraft water will just keep flowing so one bucket will last forever.

PROPERTIES OF MATERIALS

The materials we choose to build with have different properties that can work together with great results.

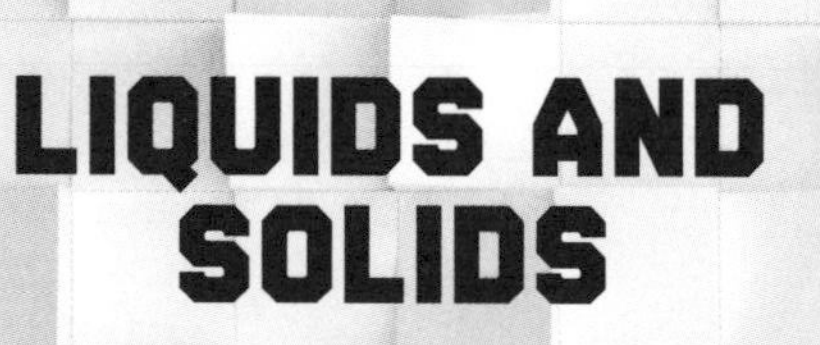

LIQUIDS AND SOLIDS

Water is a liquid, but all the other parts of your building are solid. Solid materials keep their shape. They might be bendy or soft or bouncy, but they don't spread out as soon as you put them down. Liquids take the shape of their container. If you tip out a cup of water, it won't stay cup-shaped – it will make a wide, shallow puddle. Liquids can't be piled up or cut into pieces.

Even in Minecraft water flows downwards.

GRAVITY

Water always flows from a higher place to a lower place, always going downhill (or over an edge, like a waterfall).

Water follows the shape of the rocks underneath it as it flows downwards.

Water at the bottom of the slide stops flowing and fills the space available.

STEP 3

Visitors need to get to the top of the slides, so it's time to build the walls of the tower and put stairs inside. If you use different types of wood, you can build a pattern into the tower. We have used acacia and spruce plank here. Include windows to let light in so that no one trips on the stairs. Add window bars from oak fence.

STEP 4

Once the walls are in place, build stairs around the inside walls of the tower. Use quartz stair for the steps and quartz block for the landings where the stairs turn. Don't forget to leave a doorway so that people can get in.

STEP 5

It's nearly done now — time for some finishing touches. First, add some fencing and two archways around the top of the slide. Then add more fencing along the edges of each slide (you don't want any visitors falling off!) and two more archways at the bottom. Use different types of wood to add interest. We have used jungle fence for the top of the slide and oak, birch and spruce for the sides and the bottom.

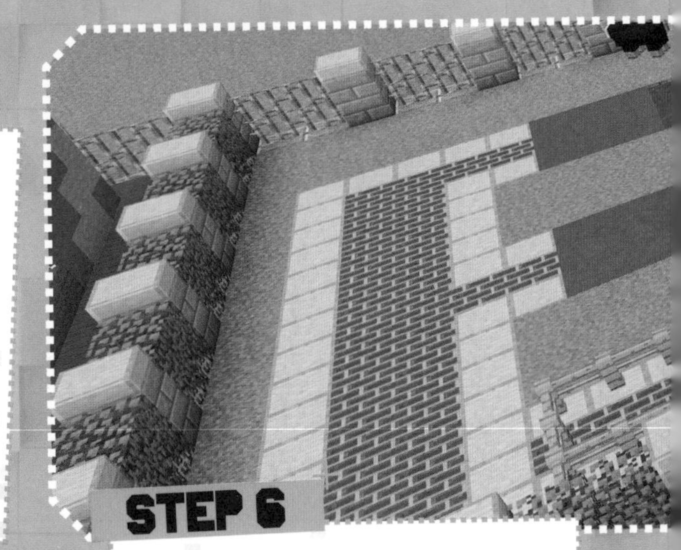

STEP 6

Last of all, finish the paving at the end of the slide and down the side with bricks and stone slab. Add oak fence to keep the queue in order. Then build a perimeter fence in the same style as the theme park perimeter fence using stone brick, stone slab, iron bar and birch leaves.

HAUNTED HOUSE

What better place to chill out after all that bouncing and sliding than a spooky, haunted house? On second thoughts, it might not be so relaxing...

SPOOKY CENTRAL

The haunted house is right in the middle of the theme park. It casts a dark shadow over the fun and games, daring your visitors to step inside. There's more going on inside than you can see from the outside. You'll need to dig a dungeon (what creepy house doesn't have a dungeon?) and separate the rooms above ground. Who knows what visitors will bump into once they are inside?

WHAT ON EARTH?

Building usually starts in the dirt, but have you ever really thought about what mud is made of, or what builders do with the mud they dig up from the ground?

DIG THE DIRT

The blocks you remove when you dig down are soil, covered with grass. In the real world, soil is a mix of tiny stones, rotting and broken down plant matter, animal waste and tiny microscopic organisms (living things), all held together with some water. It's more complicated – and important – than it looks.

shovel

grass block

THE VOLUME OF A HOLE

In Minecraft, soil just disappears if you dig it out. But if someone was really building an underground dungeon, they would have to dig out the soil and move it somewhere or pile it up. The volume of soil removed will be the same as the volume of the hole. You can work out the volume of soil removed to make your dungeon by dividing it into 3D rectangular shapes (cuboids) and working out the volume of each. You could divide this dungeon into three parts: the main room, the short, narrow passageway, and the wider area by the ladder. The volume is:

height x width x length

Add the volume of all three areas together to get the total volume of the dungeon (or the soil) you have removed.

STEP 1

Using the plan on page 27 as a guide, dig a dungeon with an exit at one end. Make it four blocks deep – the lowest level will be paved and the dungeon walls will be three blocks high.

Pave the floor with polished andesite. Line the walls with a mix of stone brick, mossy stone brick and cracked stone brick. Add a ladder at the end of the passageway.

Give each dungeon cell a 5x4 floor area and add cobwebs, a bed and slime. Use iron bar, stone brick and an iron door for the front of each cell and separate them with the same materials you used for the outer walls. Add torches along the walls before you start building on top.

torch

STEP 2

Using the plan on page 27 as a guide, build the footprint for your house. Use cobblestone stair and oak plank for the perimeter and dark oak plank for the floor. Make sure the dungeon exit comes up in the corner, two blocks in from the back wall and three blocks in from the side wall.

Mark out where you're going to place your inner walls with oak plank, leaving a space between each block. Build the frame for the outer walls from dark oak wood.

The short columns are nine blocks high and the taller columns are 13 blocks high. Place rows of blocks across the tops of these. The tallest columns for the main entrance are 21 blocks high.

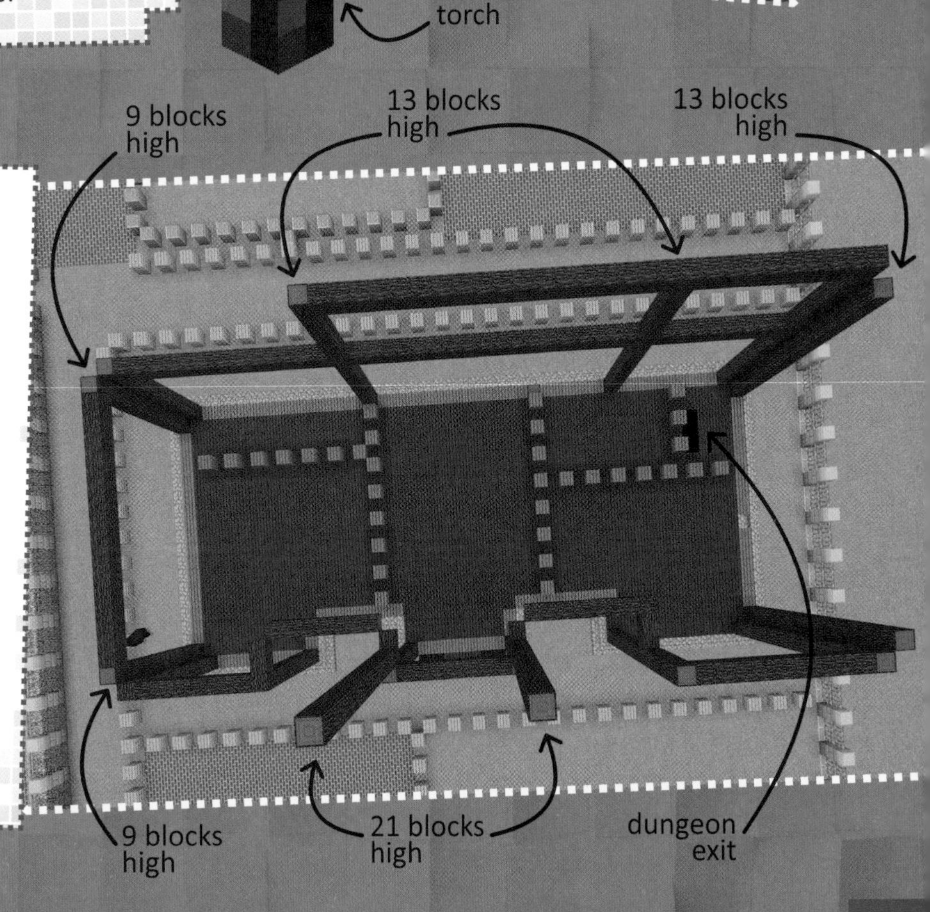

WORKING WITH NATURE

We design buildings to protect us from the elements but we use materials from nature and need to consider the environment, too.

WOODEN HOUSES

In many parts of the world, houses are made wholly or partly of wood.

They are usually built in much the same way as the haunted house, with thick, structural supports at the corners and at intervals along the walls, and then with thinner wood, like planks, filling the gaps. Wood is a thermal insulator – it helps to keep heat in. It's also light, and easy to work with as it can be cut with just a saw. Although it's not as strong as brick or stone and it burns easily, wood is a sustainable resource, so that's good for the environment.

birch wood

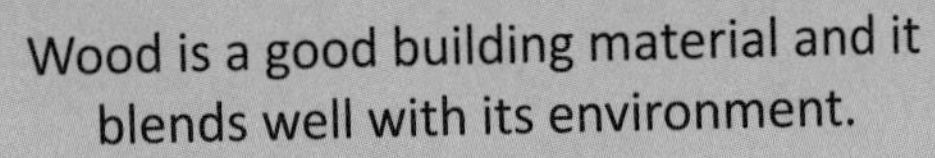
Wood is a good building material and it blends well with its environment.

WEATHERPROOF

When building a real house, builders try to get the roof on as soon as possible to stop rain falling into the house. They finish the outside walls, and any important inside structural walls, then add the roof. Internal walls and doors, the plumbing, electricity, plastering and painting are done when the roof is on and the house is secure and dry. In Minecraft, you can carry on building in the rain without any of your materials spoiling or your workers grumbling!

A roof makes a house weatherproof and keeps heat inside.

STEP 3

Fill in the walls using spruce wood plank. Leave space for a door and three windows at the front. Look back at the picture of the house on page 26 to see. One window is above the door, 10 blocks up, and the other two are at the sides, one block up. Fill them with light grey stained glass pane. In the kitchen, lay a patterned floor of black and white tiles using coal block and polished diorite.

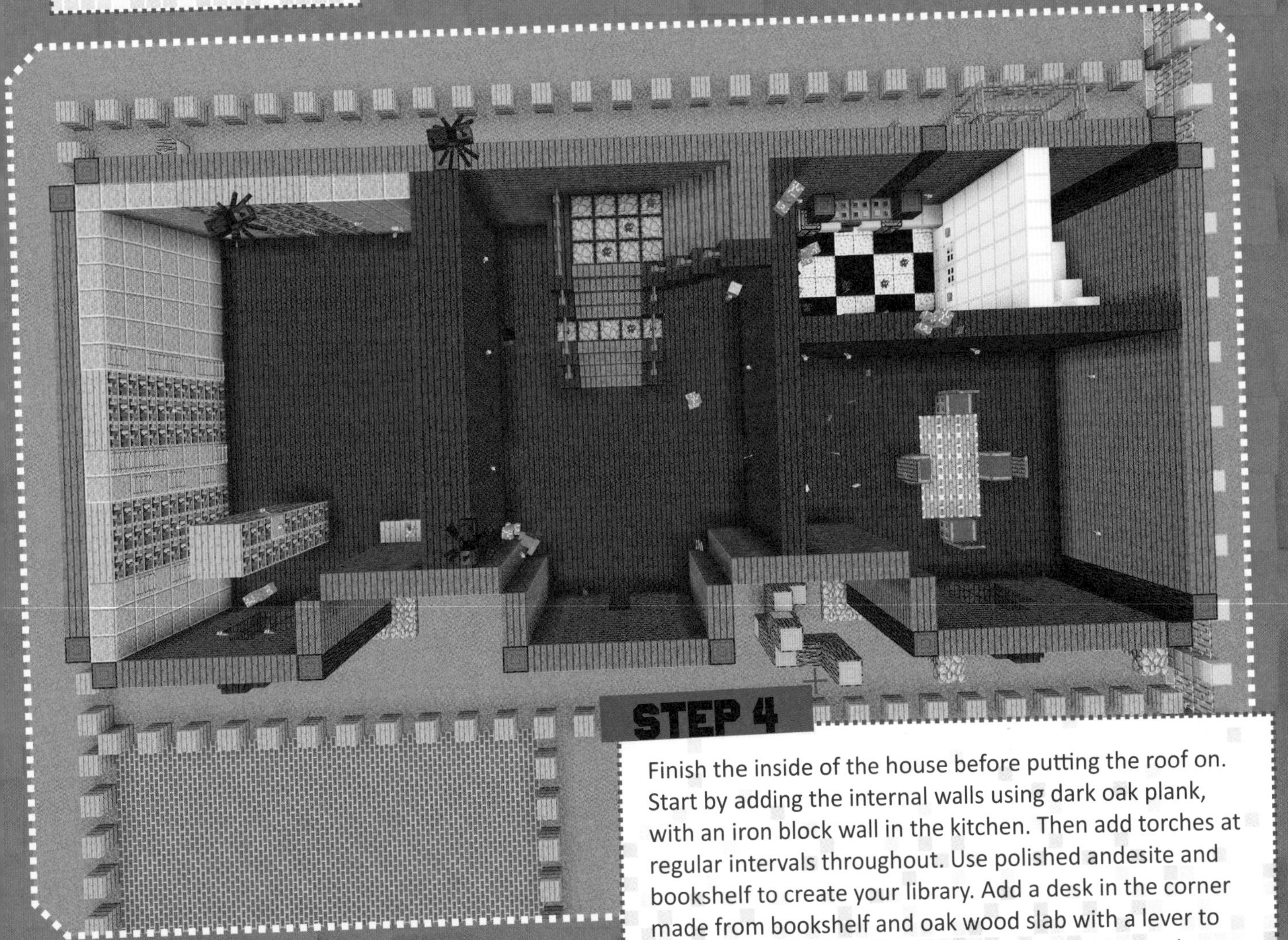

STEP 4

Finish the inside of the house before putting the roof on. Start by adding the internal walls using dark oak plank, with an iron block wall in the kitchen. Then add torches at regular intervals throughout. Use polished andesite and bookshelf to create your library. Add a desk in the corner made from bookshelf and oak wood slab with a lever to open the iron door next to it. (When you add your doors later, make sure they are all made from iron to keep the mobs contained.)

WORKING UNDER PRESSURE

Pistons are versatil in Minecraft but they are usually part of an engine, not a table!

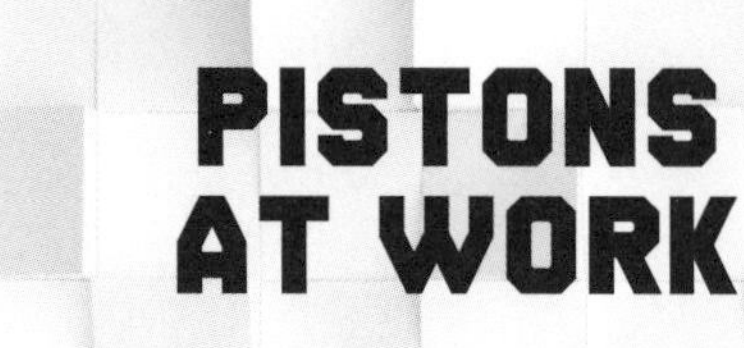

PISTONS AT WORK

Pistons live inside a cylinder in an engine within, for example, a car. They move backwards and forwards very quickly when pressure is put on them.

This pressure comes from expanding gas, which usually comes from burning fuel, such as petrol.

When the pistons move backwards and forwards, they turn a crankshaft which is connected to the car's wheels. The movement of the crankshaft is transferred to the wheels and the car moves.

piston

crankshaft

These four pistons inside a car's cylinder move up and down, which turns the crankshaft and makes the wheels move.

Minecraft piston

piston

crankshaft

STEP 5

In the dining room, remove 3x5 floor blocks in the centre of the room and put pistons in their place to make a table. Then make four chairs from spruce door (for the back), red wool (for the seat) and trapdoors (for the sides). On the wall, hang some redstone torches and some paintings – the spookier the better!

TOP TIP!

Paintings are chosen randomly, but if you get one that's too cheerful, just remove it and try again – you might get something more sinister the next time.

STEP 6

In the kitchen, add a stone slab counter along one wall with crafting tables and an anvil. Add a shelf above this made from dark oak wood and trapdoors, and build more shelving to the side of this from the same materials. Opposite the counter, place four furnaces next to a sink made from a cauldron with a lever as a tap. Finally, add redstone torches, and add some redstone dust to the floor for gruesome decoration. Behind the iron block wall, add snow blocks to create a freezer.

STEP 7

Next build the stairs in the hallway. Starting eight blocks from the back wall, build your staircase up until it's four blocks high and touching the back wall, then turn the corner and build it up another four blocks. Use spruce stair for the steps and dark oak plank and spruce fence for the sides of the stairs. Use cobblestone slab for the landings with a sprinkling of redstone dust.

STEP 8

At the top of your stairs build a floor made of spruce wood plank. Then create a row of sleeping areas, using red sandstone, oak fence, oak wood, beds and wool. Create a storage area for your double chests using wood trapdoor and acacia door. Finally create a window at the end of the bedroom, facing out of the front of the house. Glaze it with light-grey stained glass.

STEP 9

Before you start laying your roof, use spruce wood plank to build the walls up into central points. Then lay nether brick stair in diagonal rows to create the roof. Knock out a cross-shaped window at the front of the house above the window and glaze it with light grey stained glass.

STEP 10

Add corbels (wall supports) using cobblestone stair. Build a balcony on the right-hand side of the house from cobblestone slab, cobblestone stair and spruce wood plank. Use dark oak plank, stair and fence to frame your windows. Frame your iron front door with cobblestone stair, block and dark oak plank and replace the cobblestone stair at the base with nether brick stair.

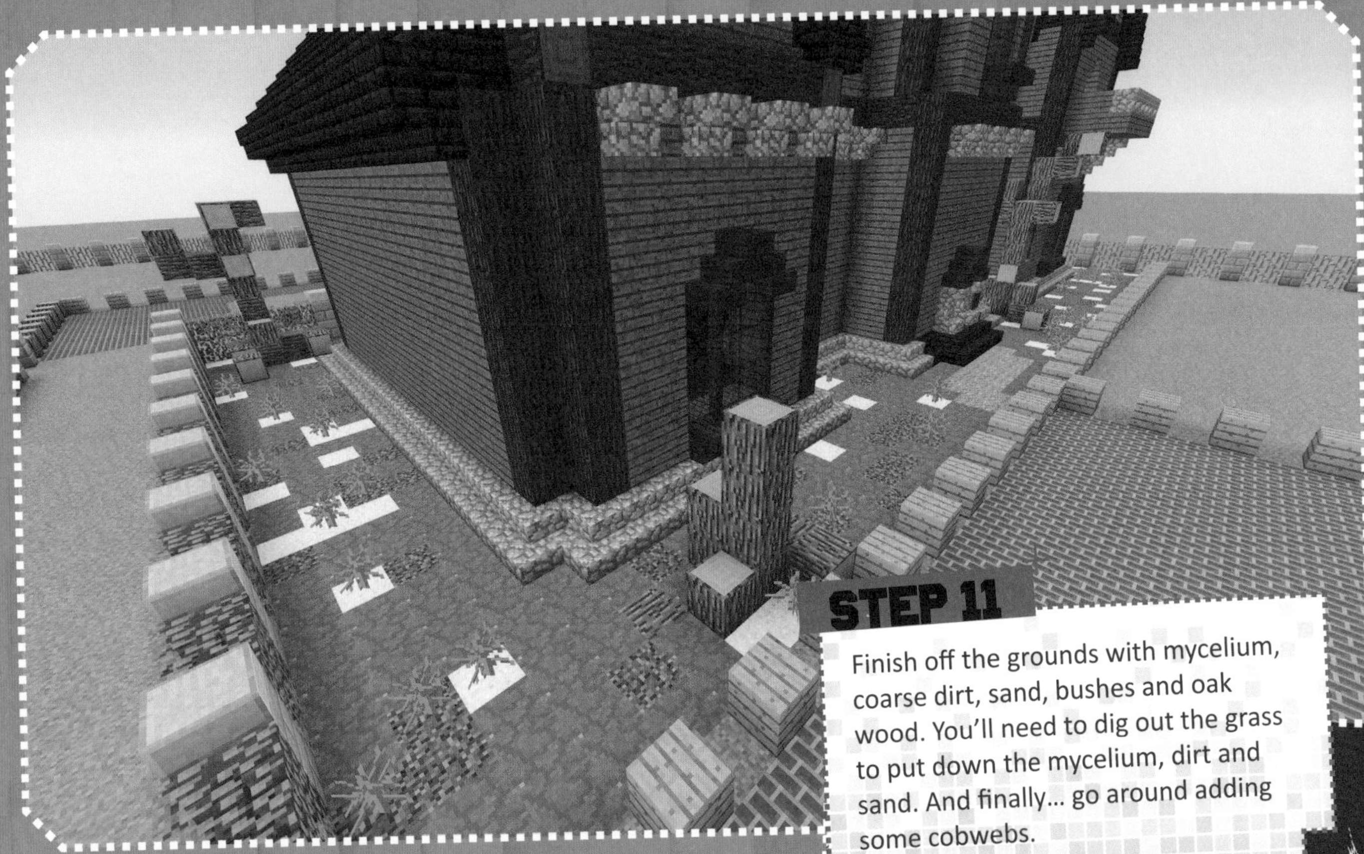

STEP 11

Finish off the grounds with mycelium, coarse dirt, sand, bushes and oak wood. You'll need to dig out the grass to put down the mycelium, dirt and sand. And finally... go around adding some cobwebs.

JUST ADD MOBS

If you want to make your haunted house even scarier, you can spawn some terrifying zombies and skeletons inside. To make sure they stay inside, put fences over all the windows, and switch your doors for iron doors. Even then, more zombies will spawn in the park when it gets dark. To keep your visitors safe – and only scared when they're in the haunted house – add redstone lamps and daylight sensors all around the outside of the house and the perimeter of the park.

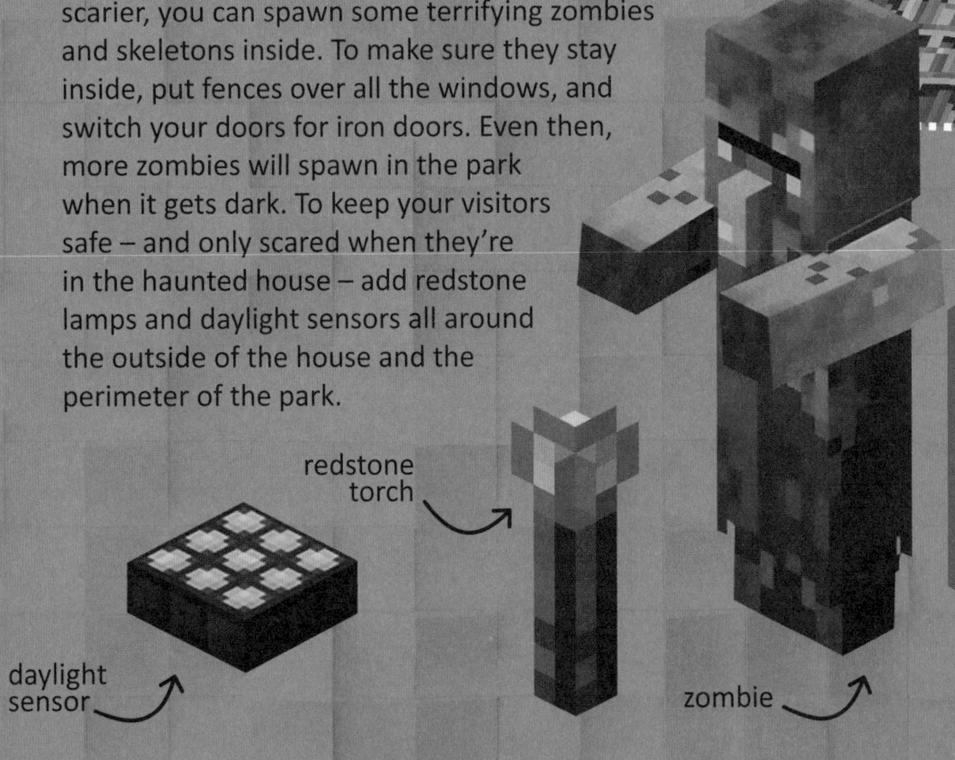

redstone torch

daylight sensor

zombie

TOP TIP!

If you want to have fun without too much fighting, select Peaceful or Low in Survival mode. Otherwise give Normal a go! If it all gets too much, you can always switch to an easier level.

FERRIS WHEEL

A Ferris wheel is one of the star attractions of any theme park. This one gives daring passengers a great view of the water slide as they swing high in the pods.

dark blocks show where connecting rows go

7
3
3
16
10
10
3
3
16
7
3
7
16
3
3
10
10
16
3
3
7

SNEAK PREVIEW

This is what your finished Ferris wheel will look like – it will be a fun ride! You'll build it in stages:

- the main wheel
- the pods
- the support structures
- the paving and barriers

TOP TIP!

The Ferris wheel goes behind the haunted house. Look back at the plan on page 11 to make sure you build it in the right place.

UNREAL!

This time, we're not starting to build on the ground but beginning in the air!

Your Ferris wheel is made from two wheels of iron block spaced three blocks apart. Use the plan on the opposite page to help you construct the circumference and spokes of the wheel, five blocks from the ground. Then, three blocks to one side of the wheel you have just built, construct another identical wheel.

SUPPORTING ROLE

Engineers and builders have to think carefully about shape, materials and how they support a structure as they build it.

WORKING WITH IRON

The main structure of the Ferris wheel is made of iron. Iron is a strong metal. It's usually made into steel, which is iron mixed with a little carbon. Steel doesn't rust, so it's better than iron for making structures like bridges (and Ferris wheels) that need to stay strong for many years. Iron was one of the earliest metals used by humans: it was first used more than 5,000 years ago.

iron block

FIRST THINGS FIRST

In real life, a structure like the Ferris wheel and its pods would be delivered in parts to be bolted together on site. Real builders would construct a framework before they built the wheel – their wheel won't hang in mid-air like yours!

Scaffolding creates a protective framework for builders and it supports a building as it grows.

GOING IN CIRCLES

The wheel is a circle. The distance across the circle, going through the middle, is called the diameter. Half the diameter is called the radius. All the lines that go from side to side through the centre of a circle are the same length.

A circle is a full turn of 360 degrees. We've divided the circle into eight equal portions, so there is an angle of $360 \div 8 = 45$ degrees between the spokes.

STEP 2

Build the 16 connecting rows that your pods will hang from, using the plan on page 36 to help you position them, and join the circles at the central axle. Attach a pod roof to the middle of each row. Make the roof from a jungle plank block surrounded by jungle wood stairs and slabs (see below). Connect the roof to the seating area with birch fence. Make the seating area from dark oak and lapiz lazuli with a birch fence safety gate. Place two jungle stairs at the bottom of the pod. Now remove the marker blocks at the base of the wheel.

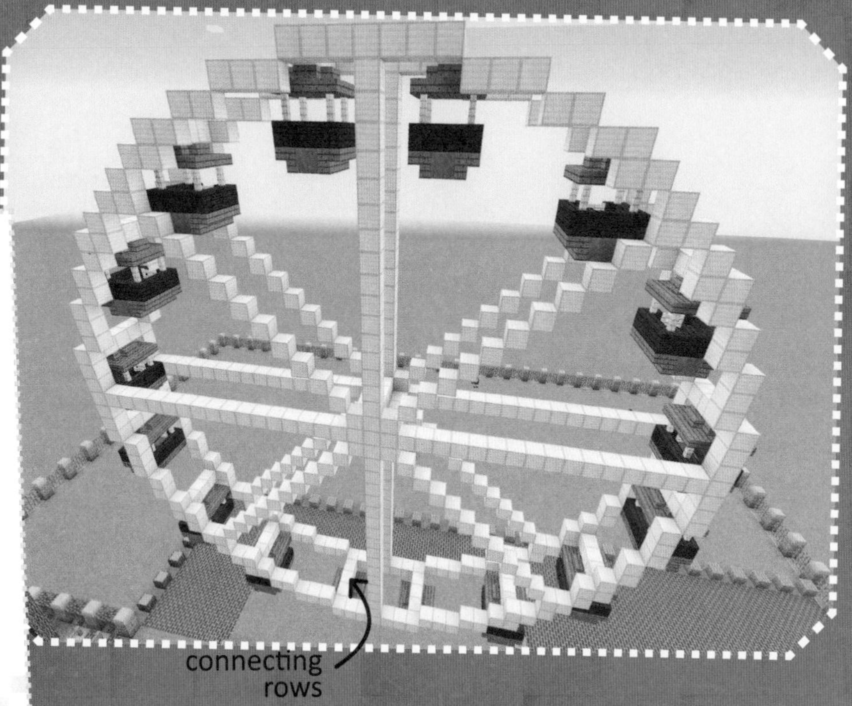

connecting rows

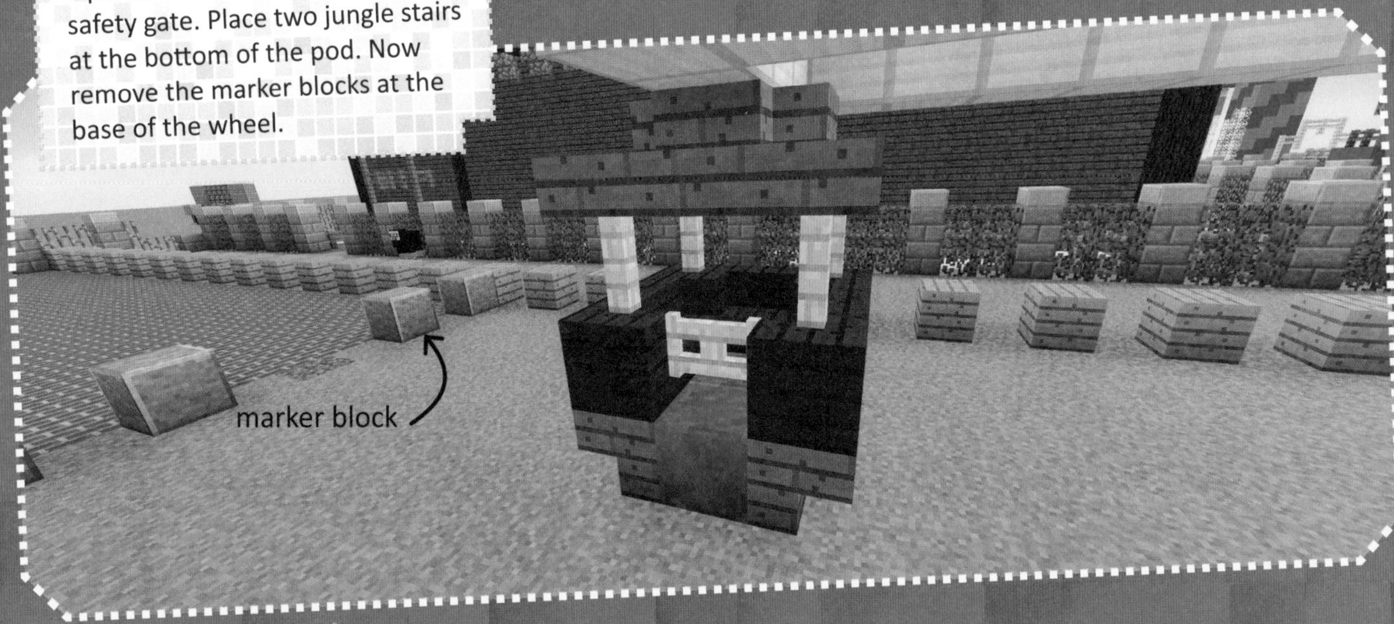

marker block

STEP 3

Add some reinforcement to the wheels to stop the spokes bending out of shape. Use different coloured wool to build two supporting circles on either side of your wheel. Start this six blocks out from the central hub along each vertical and horizontal beam.

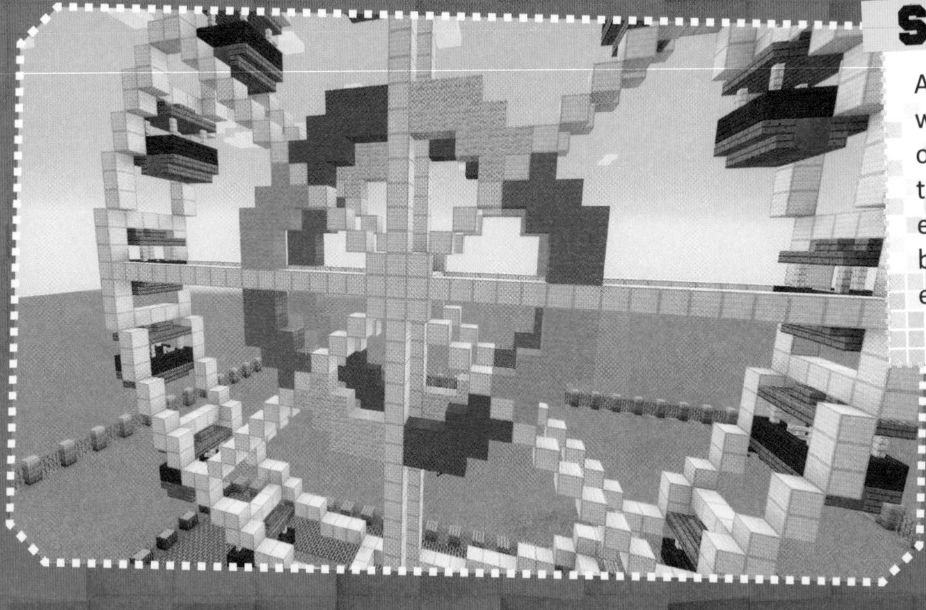

SUPER STRUCTURES

The strength of a structure depends on its shape as well as the materials it's made from. Some shapes make more stable structures than others.

STRONG AND WEAK SHAPES

This ancient Egyptian pyramid is strong because of its triangular shape.

A triangle is a strong shape. Pushing on one side does not easily distort the triangle. But pushing on one side of a square or rectangle can distort it into a parallelogram. Putting an extra circle inside the large circle of the Ferris wheel gives the spokes extra stability and makes it harder for the wheel to bend.

Force is spread evenly between the three sides of a triangle.

Force is spread evenly around a circle's whole shape.

Squares can be made stronger by adding a diagonal to form two triangles.

WHEELS AND AXLES

A Ferris wheel has at its heart a very simple machine, a wheel and an axle. The axle is a rod going through the centre of the wheel. As the axle turns, it turns the whole wheel. While the axle turns through just a short distance, the outer edge of the wheel travels a much larger distance.

The large wheels surrounding these axles mean trains can travel further faster.

STEP 4

Now we need to anchor the wheel on the ground. Use chiselled stone brick and purpur stair to make the two supporting legs that stretch from the ground to the hub of the wheel on each side.

STEP 5

Replace the grass blocks under the wheel with sea lantern, so the floor glows at night! The dimensions are 24x10.

STEP 6

For lighting around the wheel, add glowstone blocks at regular intervals on both sides.

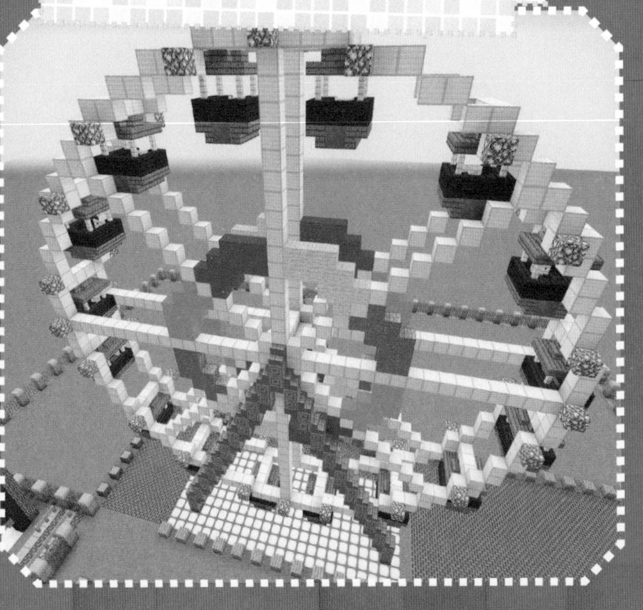

STEP 7

Dig up the grass that's left inside the area marked out for the Ferris wheel. Replace the grass with brick paving and add oak fence and cobblestone wall to make the barriers that manage the queue. Single stone slabs make the perfect steps up to the pods. Finish off your fence with birch leaves.

ROLLER COASTER

No theme park is complete without a roller coaster! This one will have your customers squealing in delight as they plummet down its steep tracks. It's at the back of the theme park, towering over everything else. Let's make it the star of the show.

PLANNING

Exactly how your roller coaster looks is up to you. You can copy ours exactly, or you can design your own swoops and loops and plunges. If you want to sketch it out first, use a piece of graph paper and draw the design you want. Then colour in each square that the line crosses. This will help you to transfer your ideas to Minecraft as it converts your curve to a series of short straight lines that correspond to blocks.

TOP TIP!

This is an aerial view of our roller coaster. Your track might be different, but you will need to put the landing and control booth in the same place as we have.

FAIRGROUND PHYSICS

Roller coasters thrill us, test our engineering skills and teach us more about physics than any other fairground ride. Read on to find out more...

FAST AND SLOW

A minecart travelling down a steep slope will go much more quickly than a minecart travelling down a shallow slope, and it will accelerate (speed up) as it goes. Then, as it climbs up a slope, a minecart will decelerate (slow down). Think about how to mix steep and shallow slopes to give your customers the most exciting ride.

minecart

VELOCITY AND ACCELERATION

Real roller coaster engineers would need to think about velocity (speed) and acceleration. Velocity measures how far something travels between two points over a fixed period of time, e.g. kilometres per hour (km/h), or metres per second (m/s). Acceleration measures an increase in velocity. If the car gets quicker and quicker, increasing its velocity by 2 metres every second, its acceleration is 2 metres per second (written 2m/s). A car going at 10 m/s that accelerates at 2 m/s^2 for 4 seconds, will be going at 18 m/s by the end of that time because the velocity increases by 2 m/s every second.

DEFYING GRAVITY

Just like the Ferris wheel and the water slide, this build starts with a bit of building that couldn't happen in real life: setting up the basic route of the roller coaster, snaking up and down through the air, unsupported!

A roller coaster's steep downward slopes increase acceleration.

STEP 1

Use spruce wood plank to trace out the route your roller coaster will follow. As long as it doesn't stretch outside the ground area allocated to the ride, it can have as many ups, downs, turns and twists as you like. Our roller coaster has three spirals and five drops! Remember that it has to be a complete circuit, so the beginning and end must join up in a single, continuous loop. Make it just one block wide — it will be more thrilling for your customers if they're right near the edge!

TOP TIP!

Your route must be solid and not have any flimsy corners, so double up the blocks underneath where necessary to make a stronger-looking base for the track.

STEP 2

Now lay track all along the top surface of the path you've made. You will need to use two types of rails: powered and unpowered rails. Use unpowered rails on downhill sections, as gravity will pull the minecarts down the slope. On uphill sections, use a mix of rail and powered rail. The steeper the slope, the more quickly your minecarts will slow down, so you will need more powered rail to boost them and get them to the top.

STEP 3

Each section of powered rail needs a source of power. Add oak plank, topped with a redstone torch at the start of each section of powered rail. This provides power directly to the rail, and up to nine rails connected to it.

UPS AND DOWNS

Minecraft minecarts behave differently on powered and unpowered rails.

On unpowered rails, a minecart moves if it is pushed forwards or if gravity pulls it downwards. If a minecart has to move uphill, it slows down and eventually stops, as it runs out of momentum.

On powered rails that are turned on, a minecart will move forwards, even uphill. But if the powered rail is turned off, it slows down any minecarts moving along it. This means you need powered track to boost your minecarts to get up the slopes and then unpowered track lets them whizz down freely, relying on gravity.

Skateboarders use momentum to reach the top of ramps.

MOMENTUM AND FRICTION

A moving object has momentum – it keeps moving in the same direction. If you push a toy car across the floor, it will keep going until it stops naturally or until it runs into something.

The reason the toy car stops naturally after a while is because the wheels of the car and the floor rub against each other – this is called friction.

The smoother two surfaces are, the less friction operates between them. You slip on ice because it's very smooth, so there is little friction between the ice and your shoes. You aren't likely to slip on gravel as there is a lot of friction between that surface and your shoes.

On a roller coaster, the speed the car gains travelling downhill gives it enough momentum to get up at least part of the next slope. Momentum won't carry it far, though, so you will need powered rails for a longer uphill ride.

This roller coaster train gains momentum as it drops down a slope.

STEP 4

A ride that just wriggles through the air looks unstable and will be way too scary! Let's add some supports to hold the track up. Use oak fence to fill in all the gaps between the track and the ground, adding oak wood columns with a gap of five blocks between each. Now it's starting to look more like a roller coaster!

STEP 5

Safety is important on a roller coaster. Add a total of four access poles made from columns of oak wood around the roller coaster's upward and downward spirals. Next to the start of the ride, connect the access poles to the roller coaster with oak fence. Add powered rail to give the minecarts an extra push as they level out at the top of the upward spiral.

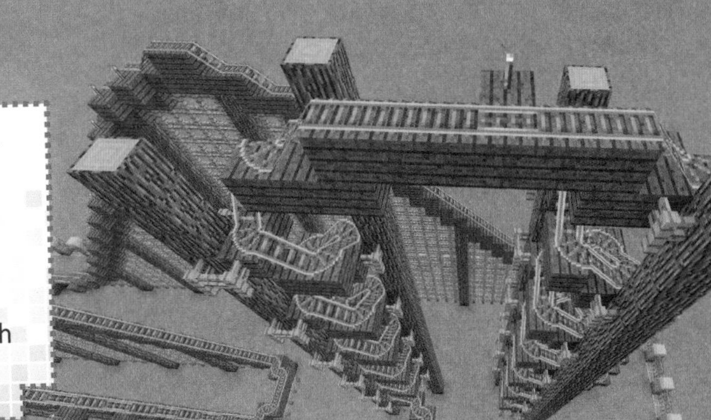

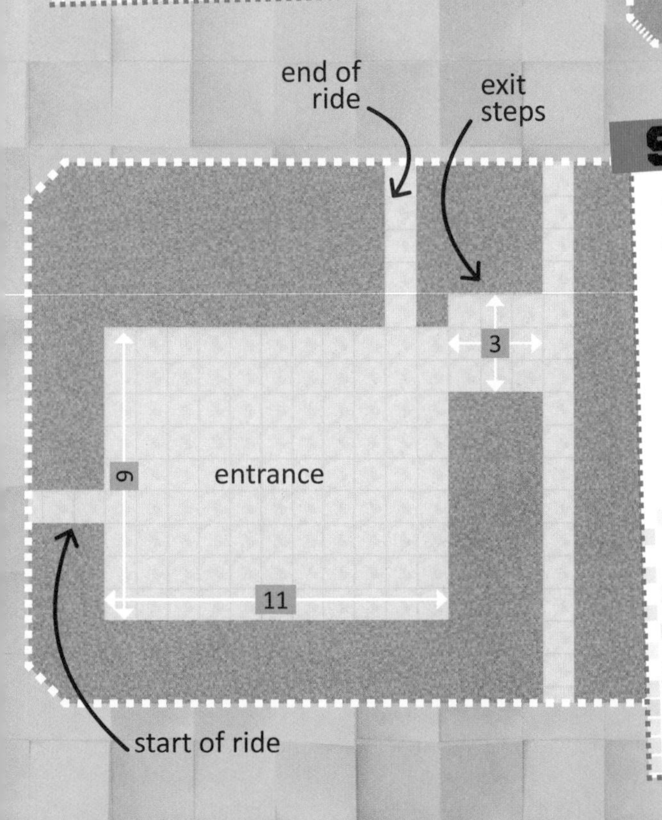

STEP 6

Next to the start of the ride, dig a pit. In the pit, put a redstone comparator, an oak pressure plate and a redstone torch. Connect them all up to the rails with redstone wire. Then cover everything with grass and put back the section of track you removed. Then, when the customer treads on the pressure plate, it cancels the signal to the comparator. This makes the cart go backwards round the curve, and then move back on to the roller coaster ride where it can be used again by another customer.

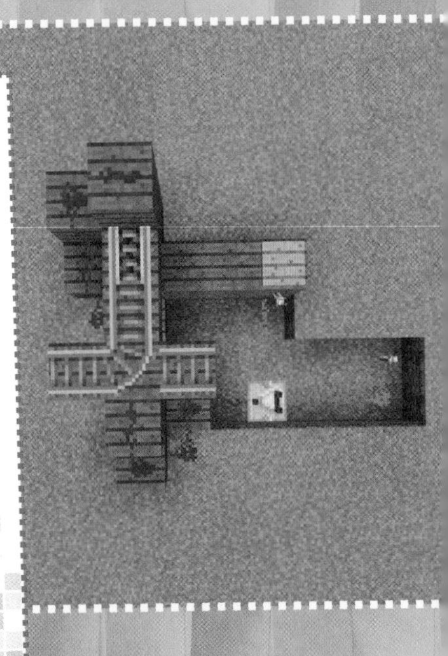

POWERING UP

Electricity can only flow through a completed circuit. A circuit needs a source of power (such as a battery, or the mains electrical supply), and wires to conduct electricity. Wires connect the source of power to the device that will do work in the circuit — like a light bulb, or a buzzer.

As soon as the components are connected, electricity flows and the light comes on, or the buzzer makes a noise. You can add a switch to make it easy to stop and start the flow of electricity. The switch works by breaking the circuit (when it's turned off) and completing the circuit (when it's turned on). In the roller coaster, you need to stop the cars moving so that people can get in or out, so a switch is vital.

redstone block

redstone repeater

daylight sensor

redstone wire

redstone torch

oak pressure plate

WHEELS ON ROADS AND RAILS

If you look at the tyres of a bicycle or car, you will see that they have a pattern on them, called tread. This increases the friction with the road surface so that the wheels don't slide around, especially when it's wet. When a vehicle goes on rails, engineers aim for as little friction as possible between the wheels and the rails. At the same time, it's important that the wheels stay on the rails. The solution is wheels with flanges. The flange sticks down on one side of the wheel, so that side can't lift up and go over the rail. As there are flanges on opposite sides of each pair of wheels, the vehicle can't easily fall to either side.

The flange on the edge of this steam train wheel keeps it on the track.

STEP 7

With all the track in place, it's time to build the entrance where people will get into the minecarts. Build this over the top of the control panel you've just made. Use jungle wood plank for the walls, spruce stair for seating on the other side of the track and spruce slab for the roof. Complete it with cobblestone wall columns at the front and a stone button on the central column at the back that you can press to start the ride.

STEP 8

Use stone slab and bricks to pave the ground. Add oak fence and organize the queuing area. This is going to be a popular ride, so we've set aside a large area for people to wait. Make sure alternate rows of fence go right to the wall to stop eager customers queue-jumping! At the end of the ride, create an exit path starting with oak wood stair steps and edged with cobblestone wall. Finally, add minecarts to the track.

minecart

ANIMAL ZONE

A theme park can be a bit full-on with all those exciting rides, so how about giving your customers somewhere calming to relax? The animal zone is just that – a place to chill with some friendly beasts.

ZOO OVERVIEW

Here's the basic layout for the animal zone. Each enclosure is rectangular, but otherwise it is adapted to suit the needs of the type of animal that will live in it.

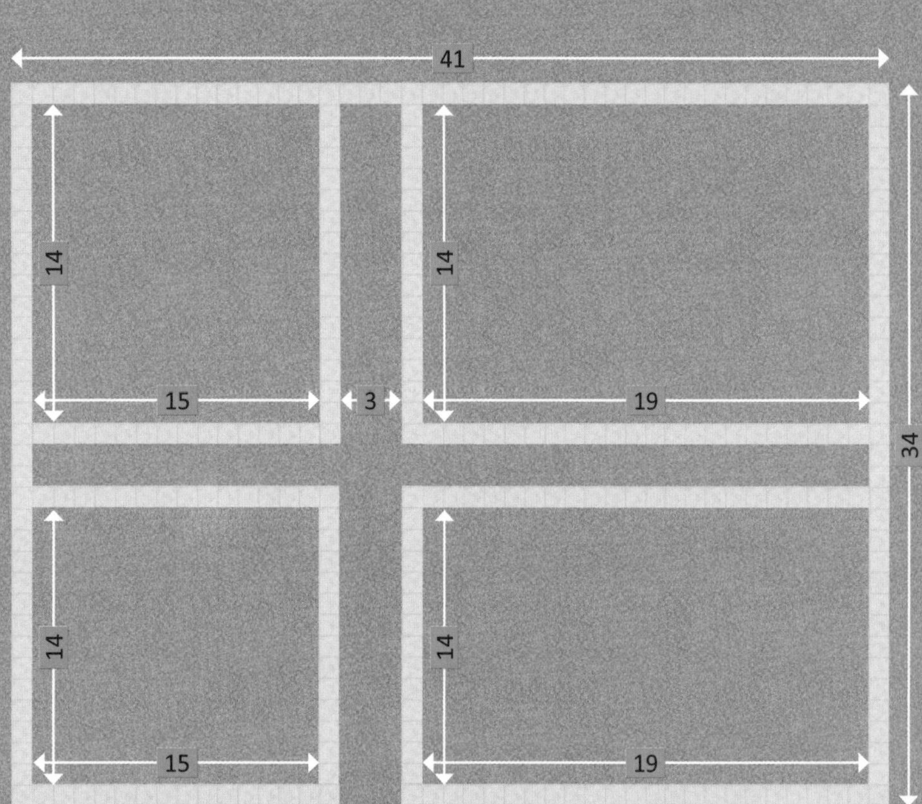

ROOM WITH A MOO

There will be two larger enclosures, one for the horses and one for the cows, and two slightly smaller areas, one for the sheep and chickens and one for the rabbits.

NATURAL SELECTION

We've used farm animals, but you could pick different animals and change the enclosures to suit your choices.

PLANNING FOR LIFE

All the other builds have been planned to make it fun, safe and easy for visitors to use the theme park. But animals are living things too, so we must to their needs into account. They all need:

- food
- water
- a safe, dry place to live.

But different types of animals also have specific needs. They need different environments (surroundings) that reflect the places they are usually found in the wild, and different types of food. You wouldn't keep polar bears and lions in the same type of environment, for example. Lions live in the hot grasslands of Africa, but polar bears live in the cold snow and ice of countries near the North Pole.

fish

raw beef

hay bale

water bucket

LOOK OUT!

Some animals eat other animals and are fierce predators. It's safe to mix some types of animals, but others might hurt each other, either on purpose or accidentally, perhaps by treading on them. You also need to make sure your animals will be kept safely enclosed by the barriers you use. You don't want them wandering all over the theme park!

STEP 1

Start by laying rows of mossy cobblestone wall to mark out the walls of all four enclosures. Use the plan on page 51 for the positions of the cobblestone wall.

TOP TIP!

In Survival mode, mobs sometimes escape through fence. Keep the same look but improve security by adding a layer of glass pane around the outside of your fence.

glass pane

STEP 2

Complete the walls of the horse enclosure using mossy cobblestone wall. Build them four blocks high with columns placed five blocks apart. Create a pattern by leaving two sections of wall hanging down and one pointing up between each column. These gaps allow people to see the animals from outside.

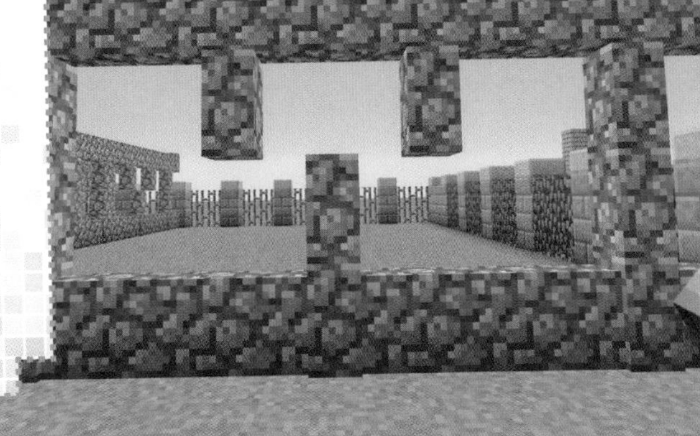

STEP 3

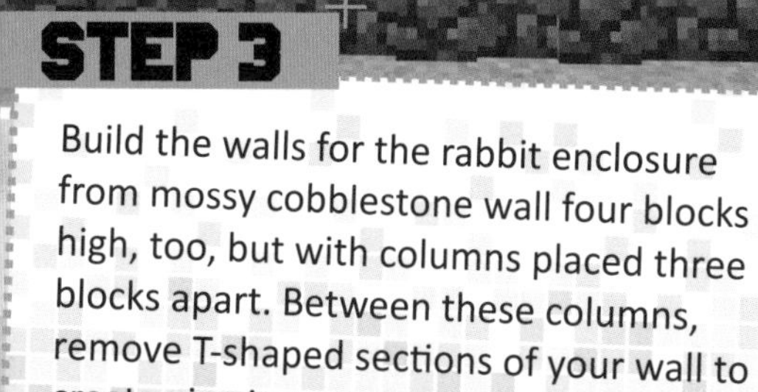

Build the walls for the rabbit enclosure from mossy cobblestone wall four blocks high, too, but with columns placed three blocks apart. Between these columns, remove T-shaped sections of your wall to create viewing windows.

STEP 4

Construct the walls for the sheep and chickens' enclosure by placing mossy cobblestone wall in a zigzag pattern. Make each diagonal zig (or zag!) four blocks high and three blocks across. When you're done there should be lots of upside down, T-shaped viewing windows.

STEP 5

Space the columns in the walls of the cows' enclosure two blocks apart, with lazy figure-of-eight shapes removed to make the viewing windows.

FOOD AND FEEDING

All living things need food, and at the bottom of the food chain, supporting everything, are plants. Learn how to grow them, and you'll be able to look after all your animals.

HAY FOR HERBIVORES

Most of the animals in the animal zone are herbivores: that means that they eat plants. Lots of animals are herbivores, including many mammals, birds, insects and fish. Elephants, squirrels, parrots, snails and caterpillars are all herbivores. They eat leaves, fruit, nuts and seeds from plants. Other animals eat meat – other animals. They are called carnivores. Lions, dogs, sharks and vultures are carnivores. And some animals can eat plants or animals. They are called omnivores. Pigs and some monkeys are omnivores.

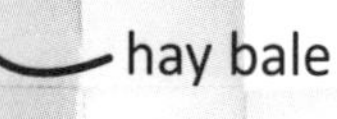

hay bale

ENTER THE ANIMALS!

In Minecraft, all animals can be spawned from one of their spawn eggs, but in real life animals either give birth to live babies or lay eggs. Birds and reptiles lay eggs. Most mammals give birth to babies. Some fish give birth and others lay eggs.

spawn egg

GROWING PLANTS

Plants need several things to grow properly. They need water, sunlight, and soil with the right kind of nutrients. To help plants to grow, farmers and gardeners often add fertiliser to the soil. This works like extra food for the plants. One type of fertiliser is bone meal, made of ground-up animal bones. Bones are rich in the element phosphorous, which is vital for plants.

poppy

BABY GROWTH

Some baby animals can eat the same food as adult animals as soon as they are born or hatched. Mammals produce milk to feed their young. Other animals chew up or partly digest food before feeding it to their babies. Lots of birds do this.

STEP 6

It's no use having an enclosure that no one can get into! Put a gate in the wall of each enclosure using dark oak fence gate. It should be three blocks in from the crossroads at the centre of the animal zone. Leave space above the gate for head room so that people can fit through!

STEP 7

Horses eat hay, so pile some hay bales up in one corner of their enclosure. And, like all animals, horses need fresh water to drink. Put three cauldrons in another corner and fill them with water. Then spawn your horses!

STEP 8

Next to the horse enclosure, build two chicken coops, using birch wood for the walls and oak stair for the roof. Add a row of birch stair across the bottom of the coops to keep the chickens off the ground at night. Don't forget an oak door so it's easy for park workers to go inside and clean the chicken coops. Add birch plank above it for decoration. The sheep and chickens need water to drink. Dig a pond (just two blocks deep so that it's not too dangerous) and edge it with some blocks of sand, set into the ground. Finally, sprinkle some bone meal to make the grass and some extra flowers grow. Then spawn your sheep and chickens.

TOP TIP!

Feed your chickens watermelon, wheat or pumpkin seeds and shut them away in their coop at night to keep them safe!

TIME TO REPRODUCE

Happy, well-fed animals will eventually start to make babies. Different types of animals do this in different ways, in the real world as well as in Minecraft...

BIRDS VS MAMMALS

Although real chickens come from eggs, cows, sheep, horses and rabbits are all mammals. Mammals carry their babies inside them and give birth to them. Birds, reptiles and some types of fish lay eggs.

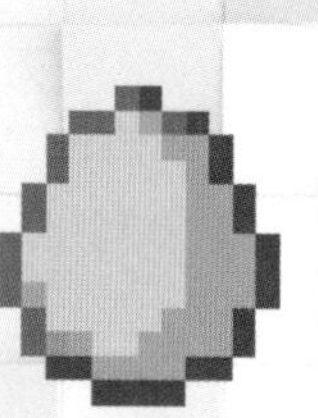

GOOD BREEDING

To encourage passive or tame mobs to breed, offer them food. When heart particles appear, mobs are in love mode. Two animals of the same type will come together as long as they are not more than eight blocks apart. Then, after a few seconds, a baby of the same type will appear.

In the real world, animals tend to breed in spring or the start of the rainy season when warmer weather is on the way and plants are starting to grow. Warmth and food give their young a better chance of surviving.

THE RIGHT ENVIRONMENT

Minecraft mobs, just like real animals, reproduce in particular places. For example, horses naturally spawn in savannas or plains. Wolves only spawn in taiga biomes and polar bears, as you'd imagine, spawn in ice plains. Cows, pigs and chickens are pretty common and pop up all over the place.

In the real world, things are pretty similar, cold places with little food, like the Arctic, have fewer animals and warm places with lots of vegetation, like the Amazon, are host to lots of animal species.

Minecraft river biomes are a great place to fish.

TOP TIP!

bone meal

If you sprinkle bone meal over grass, it makes the grass grow taller (and flowers grow, too). This is very important for the sheep and chicken enclosure because sheep turn grass to dirt when they graze so you'll need to keep sprinkling bone meal there.

STEP 9

The next big enclosure is for cows. This has some landscaping, with a bit of higher ground and a tree. The cows will need a lot to drink, so dig a hole to set six cauldrons into the ground and fill them with water. To make the raised area, use grass blocks piled up and sprinkle some bone meal to add tall grass and flowers to the ground. Finally, spawn your cows.

STEP 10

Prepare the rabbit enclosure by adding some jungle wood with jungle leaves over the top of it to create some bushes where they can shelter. Dig a pond in one corner and fill it with water so that they can have a drink. Spawn your bunnies and then tap (or right click) the grass with your shovel to create paths between the enclosures.

FOR REAL!

Fertilizer makes plants grow faster in the real world. In Minecraft you can use bone meal to make saplings grow faster.

STEP 11

Sprinkle bone meal to grow flowers and tall grass. These will provide food for your bunnies, as well as somewhere for them to hide.

FINISHING TOUCHES

All your rides are ready, but before the park opens for business you need to add some finishing touches. We'll add paving, lighting, a ticket booth, a large entrance sign – and make sure people can get into and out of the rides!

THEME PARK

THINKING ABOUT ROUTES

When you have a lot of people milling around in an area, they need to be able to move to where they want to go without getting in each others' way. The entrances and exits are separate to keep people moving smoothly and safely.

NIGHT LIGHTS

Glowstone provides light during Minecraft's night. In the real world, substances that glow on their own in the dark are called phosphorescent. They absorb and store light, then release it.

Solar powered lights have a solar panel which absorbs energy from sunlight during the day. This solar energy is stored in a battery. A light sensor monitors the sunlight and triggers a switch when it goes above or below a certain level. When it gets dark, the solar powered lights turn on, using power from the battery.

Some lights powered by mains electricity also come on automatically at night, either using a light sensor or a timer.

Many different types of sensors are used to trigger automatic reactions. Security lights and car alarms have motion sensors: if something moves near the light, it turns on, or if the car is jogged or pushed, the alarm sounds. Smoke detectors have a sensor that sets off an alarm if there is smoke in the air.

daylight sensor

glowstone

STEP 1

First pave the central path inside the theme park with diorite. So far, the ground here is still covered with grass, but in a real park that would soon get churned to mud when hoards of eager customers rush in. The paved area runs from the entrance to behind the haunted house.

Around the edges of your path, add a row of andesite and glowstone blocks. Placing the glowstone every six blocks will provide ground-level lighting at night.

entrance

Now go around the whole of the path, adding entrances and exits for all the rides with glowstone blocks either side. The exit for the bouncy castle goes next to the grass that runs in front of the landing area. The entrances and exits for the other rides connect with the queuing areas and paths. We've marked where these go on the image to the right.

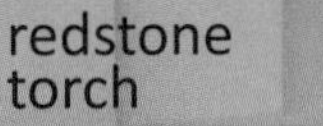

STEP 4

Now people can find their way safely along the paths. Let's add some torches so that they can see clearly when they are in the queues. Plant a torch on the end of each bit of fence in the queuing areas; add extras if you like.

STEP 5

We need a ticket booth so that people visiting the park can pay to come in. Place it in a central position at the front entrance. Make it seven blocks wide and six blocks from back to front, with stone brick walls and a roof made from spruce wood stair. Put a single row of andesite around the base. Add dark oak fence on either side up to the edge of the path.

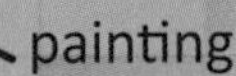

STEP 6

Now add side windows, using glass pane. To make it nicer for the person who has to work in the ticket booth, add a painting to the wall. Then place a villager inside.

TOP TIP!

At the main entrance, use signs to direct your guests towards the different attractions in the theme park. Then, outside the entrance to each attraction, put a sign with a fun name on it!

STEP 7

Finish off the theme park with a huge sign near the entrance. Make it really big so that people can see it from a long way away and it will draw in customers. This one is 30 blocks high and 24 blocks wide. Make the supports and the face of the sign from black stained clay and the frame from yellow wool. We've left the face of this sign blank so you can create your own name for it – it's your park so make your mark on it! Use more brightly coloured wool to make your lettering.

THEME PARK

STEP 8

Finally, sprinkle bone meal to add some flowers around the rides or along the fences. Or perhaps you'd like to add a few benches, more trees or more lighting. If you want to add more rides, you could take down part of the perimeter fence and extend the park. Your park could grow and grow!

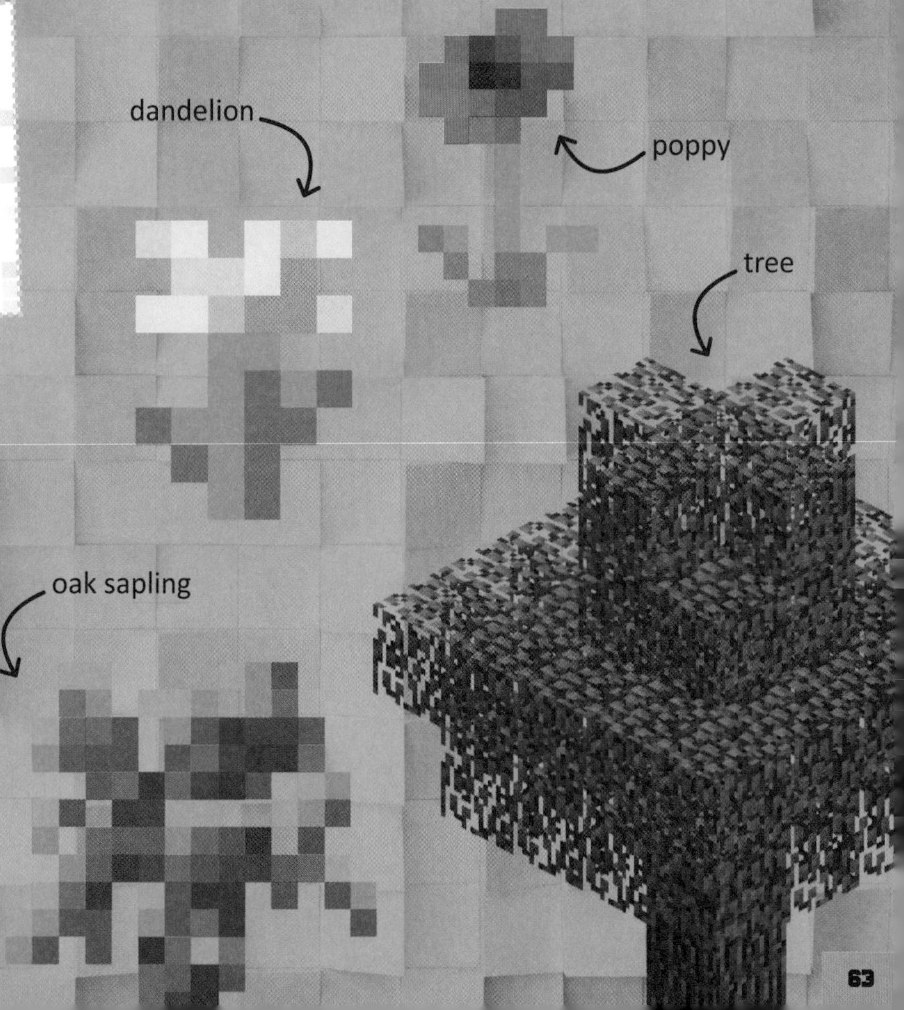

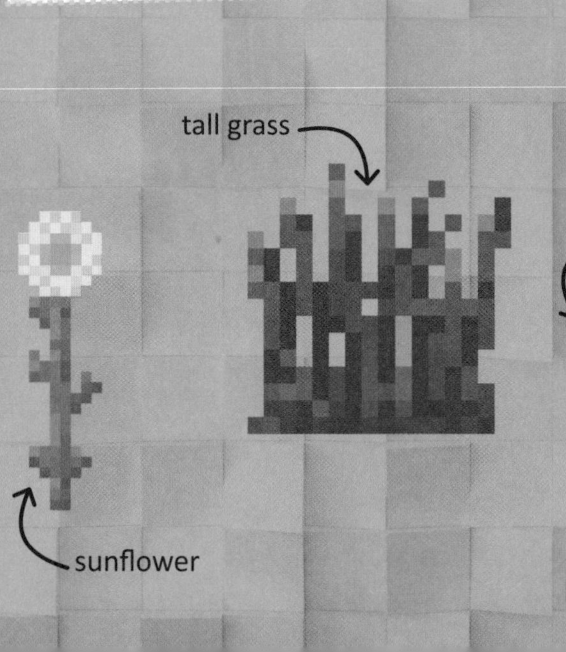

dandelion

poppy

tree

tall grass

oak sapling

sunflower

GLOSSARY

ACCELERATION
The process of getting steadily faster, building up speed.

ARCHITECT
A person whose job is to design buildings and build structures such as bridges.

CENTURY
A period of 100 years.

CIRCUIT
A closed loop of wire and other components that conduct electricity, so that a current can flow and the electricity can be used to do useful work, such as power lights.

CONDUCT (ELECTRICITY, HEAT)
To carry.

CORBEL
A structural piece of stone on a wall.

CRANKSHAFT
The part of a machine that connects to a piston, converting the backwards-and-forwards motion of the piston to a circular motion.

CYLINDER
A tube-shaped container.

DIMENSIONS
Measured sizes or distances on a plan or in the real world.

ENVIRONMENT
The natural setting in which something lives or is situated. It can refer to a local environment (such as a forest or lake) or the whole natural world, often called 'the environment'.

FLAMMABLE
Capable of being burned.

FOOD CHAIN
A series of organisms (living things) that eat one another. For example, a fox eats a rabbit which in turn eats grass.

FOOTPRINT
The area on the ground occupied or overhung by a building.

FOUNDATIONS
Buried support for a building or other structure, often consisting of walls that go into the ground and are rooted in a layer of rubble, concrete or other hard material.

FRICTION
A force acting between two surfaces that works to prevent or slow down the movement of one over the other.

MAGENTA
A purplish-pink colour.

MOMENTUM
The ability of a moving object to keep moving unless some force or object stops it.

PERIMETER
The total distance around the outside edge(s) of a shape.

PROPORTIONS
The same relative sizes of two measurements. For example, if a rectangle is twice as long as it is tall in a plan, the corresponding rectangle in a model must also be twice as long as it is tall.

SCALE
A scale of 1:10 means that one unit (centimetre, inch, mile, etc.) on a plan stands for 10 units in the real world.

SOLAR PANEL
A panel of solar cells which converts sunlight to electricity.

SOLAR POWERED
Driven with electricity converted from the energy in sunlight.

VELOCITY
Speed.

WATER-TIGHT
Capable of keeping water in or out without leaking.